Herald Express

Pub Walks
in and around
THE HALDON HILLS

Brian Carter

OBELISK PUBLICATIONS

ALSO BY THE AUTHOR
Walking "With a Tired Terrier" In and Around Torbay
Walks in the South Hams
Pub Walks in the South Hams
SOME OTHER 'WALKS' BOOKS
Diary of a Dartmoor Walker, *Chips Barber*
Diary of a Devonshire Walker, *Chips Barber*
Ten Family Walks on Dartmoor, *Sally & Chips Barber*
Ten Family Walks in East Devon, *Sally & Chips Barber*
Six Short Pub Walks on Dartmoor, *Sally & Chips Barber*
The Templer Way, *Derek Beavis*
Walks in the Shadow of Dartmoor, *Denis McCallum*
Walks in Tamar and Tavy Country, *Denis McCallum*
Walks in the Totnes Countryside, *Bob Mann*
Walks in the Chagford Countryside, *Terry Bound*
The Great Walks of Dartmoor, *Terry Bound*
Wheelchair Walks in Devon, *Lucinda Gardner*

We have over 120 Devon titles; for further details please send a 1st class stamp to Obelisk
Publications at 2 Church Hill, Pinhoe, Exeter, EX4 9ER or telephone (01392) 468556

Acknowledgements

All maps and drawings by Brian Carter
Dave Barrett for pages 11 and 25
All other photographs by Chips Barber
apart from page 4

First published in 1996 by
Obelisk Publications, 2 Church Hill, Pinhoe, Exeter, Devon
Designed by Chips and Sally Barber
Typeset by Sally Barber
Printed in Great Britain by The Devonshire Press Limited, Torquay, Devon

Introduction

HERE we are again with another walk for every day of the week between the Exe and the Teign, beginning and ending at a pub. They were done in the winter and early spring, and the winter I chose must have been one of the wettest of the century. But this only served to heighten what spring had to offer in and around the Haldon Hills. I needed no excuses, though, to make those pub pilgrimages through some of Devon's loveliest countryside.

Called to the bar back in the 1950s it's always been pleasant to combine a love of lane and footpath walking with the teasing of the tastebuds – helped by the brewers, distillers, wine and cidermakers. Drinkwise, rural Devon is still the great adventure with some of the UK's best cider beckoning like the Holy Grail – Inch's vintage, Gray's, Luscombe's, Churchward's, the orchard gold waits at the end of the rainbow, well, at the bottom of the lane anyway. I love a good walk and a good whisky, the lane that winds to the Windfall Wine, gales and ales, a pub, pint and pasty pilgrimage with fine old-fashioned Nature Study paving the

trail to the bar and the fireside. Luton, Cockwood, Chudleigh, Doddiscombsleigh, Kenton, and Dawlish Warren are stepping stones over hills, along the riverside, through coombes and other green places as varied as the weather which was mainly wet. But a surfeit of H_2O didn't dampen my enthusiasm for South Devon. Redsoil born and bred I'm fiercely proud of my roots and the quality of the local landscape. The wild-looking farmland around Doddiscombsleigh, the vision of Dartmoor seen from Little Haldon Cross; the Exe estuary, the tidal Teign, woods, meadows, sand dunes, farm, cottage and stream – in our part of the world you can walk into beauty without going very far. The longest tavern trek in this collection is 8 miles; the shortest is a 2 mile stroll high on rural calm and river views. Crossing the hills between two of Devon's loveliest rivers I saw the morning and evening flights of wild geese, heard the piping of curlew and other waders, stood under larksong, chatted to cows, found celandine gold in the rain, murk, and enjoyed a superb malt whisky at a pub with 200 whiskies on its shelves and a choice of 700 bottled wines.

Even if you choose to walk alone you'll never be lonely. Hens will be banjoing, horses will lay their chins on top of the gate and stare at you, and skylarks will offer their startling version of that great hymn of childhood 'Morning has Broken'. Of course I'm biased with redsoil on me tongue as

well as on my boots! But go and see for yourself or sit down at home and let me do the legwork ... and tilt the elbow.

Brian Carter enjoys 'a cider with Laurie Lee'

— 1 —
Places for Poets to Sing About
From the Elizabethan Inn, Luton

(Luton, Lindridge, Humber, Bishopsteignton, Little Haldon and Luton again – eight miles)
Luton can easily be reached from the main Torbay–Exeter road at various junctions, or drive along the country roads from Kingsteignton, Bishopsteignton, Teignmouth or Dawlish.

WIND, sun, clouds and showers – the late morning had all the ingredients of a typical West Country April day. So, leaving the ample car park of The Elizabethan Inn, I turned right and came down into the little village of Luton to enjoy a lane ramble in perfect walking weather. Beyond Ivy Cottage's thatch I came past the stream, Westhayes Farm was a bit farther along the road and then it was uphill into the countryside.

My route to the left was signposted Ideford but at Luton Cross, a few yards away, it was straight on signed Lindridge and Bishopsteignton.

Leaving White House behind I walked the narrow lane under pale gold oak leaves between high hedges and primrose banks. The rich red soil in the ploughed fields looked good enough to eat but the cattle by the pasture gate preferred an elevenses of hay.

Looking down on Luton from the heights of Little Haldon

Yet another crossroads sign pointed me towards Humber and Bishopsteignton, and the verges were thick with magenta flowers of campion. But the flail-mowed hedges up by Lindridge didn't go with the shimmering wheatfields and wherever Nature had been left to get on with the job of producing a classic Devon spring Alexanders shared the lane-side with other wild flowers.

At Humber Ridge House I passed a lady with two horses, one of which had plenty of feather on its fetlocks. Blackthorn blossom still showed in the hedges among the misty greens of the season all the way to the barn conversions of Humber Mill and the aubretia on the walls of Home Humber and Little Humber.

On the other side of tiny Humber Bridge a gymkhana was in progress and the cherry tree on the verge was shedding blossom. Between clouds the sun was hot and the wind kept everything on the move as it rushed and whispered through leaves, branches, grass and flowers.

At Lindridge Park and the massive pillars of the gateway I came left up past Higher Humber Farm, meeting cars, horseboxes and pony riders as I climbed the hill to Rowden Cross. Here I stopped to enjoy the sweep of the wind in the corn and that superb view of Dartmoor with some of my favourite tors sunlit.

Luton — The Elizabethan INN — Little Haldon Cross — Golf Course — Little Haldon Cross — Lindridge — Humber — Rowden Cross — Ruins of the palace — Bishopsteignton

A shower fell and up went the hood of my cagoule. Down the winding lane I loped into a view of the Teign and the patchwork fields above the estuary. The hedge tops were thick with blackthorn blossom which wasn't as white as the stitchwort on the banks.

Bishopsteignton waited below Clanage Cross. Big, leafy gardens saw me into the outskirts of the village and I came through the narrows past the Bishop John de Grandisson pub into Fore Street. Then the raised pavement brought me to the Pasty Mine bakery and the open window where I bought a hot oggie to eat on the hoof.

At the other end of the village I swung left at the Ring o'Bells and walked up Radway Hill to turn right into Radway Street. Passing little houses and cottages I arrived at the crossroads, and bore left along Old Walls Road with the farmhouse facing the calf pen. Then the row of twelve lombardy poplars saw me to the ruins of the bishop's palace which have been incorporated in the modern farm buildings.

Old Walls Hill was a long steep slog but the wildflower banks, a blue sky and white clouds would have had those wayfaring Edwardian poets singing as they puffed on their pipes and cobbled together the sonnets.

With the sun on them, oak leaves looked like golden blossom. I walked under them to a gateway view of The Ness, the Teign estuary and the Channel. The sky had cleared and all the clouds were over the sea and the moors.

Bearing left at the next cross my route ran past the bright gorse of Little Haldon Heaths to another left turn at Teignmouth Golf Club. Banks of violets below the gorse created another of those idylls Edward Thomas would have celebrated on his last spring before the First World War claimed his life.

This walk conjures up two Little Haldon Crosses and it was right at the first one to come between the conifers and the golf course to the second and one of Great Britain's great British views.

From the small car park I could look across miles of farmland to a vision of Dartmoor, with Rippon Tor, Saddle Tor and Hay Tor on the horizon. Cloud shadow swept slowly over the landscape, and the magic of blackthorn blossom,

red soil and green fields, under a huge sky, was the essence of Devon.

After soaking it up in silence I came down the long country road to Luton and The Elizabethan Inn again. The smell of cooking was probably the best sort of welcome a country pub can provide – that and the scent of woodsmoke from a stove or open fire.

In the lounge I met innkeeper Alex Latham, 16 years in residence and still as enthusiastic as ever about the hospitality business. The old wooden tables, chairs and settles, and a bar with shelves packed with interesting bottles were part of that authentic pub atmosphere that always appeals to me.

As a property the inn dates from the reign of the first Queen Elizabeth, but when Queen Victoria began off-loading pockets of land on the royal estates she decreed that the house, which is now the Elizabethan, should become a wayside tavern. The occupants had to run it as a beer and cider house. And on the Queen's command it was called The Albert.

In 1952 or 3 the name of the then Heavitree house was changed. The new owner wrote to our present queen after her coronation and got permission to rename it The Elizabethan.

Tucked away among the old cottages and farms under the Haldon Hills it's an inn for all seasons, somewhere to finish a country walk or begin an evening with good food and drink.

— 2 —
Up the Creek Without Need of a Paddle
From the Ship Inn, Cockwood

(Cockwood, Cofton Hill, Eastdon Plantation, Orchard Lane, Dawlish Warren Road and Cockwood – two miles)
Take the Dawlish Warren Road out of Dawlish and head for Cockwood. Church Road is on the left at the harbour, beyond the last house in the village. The Ship Inn is a few yards up from the village stores. From the Exeter direction follow the A379 through Starcross.

LEAVING Church Road and Cockwood Marsh I came up to Cofton Hill with the Ship Inn on my right. It was close to opening time, the sun shone and big clouds rolled over the Exe estuary.

Passing little white houses I came to a flight of steps for a view of Cockwood Harbour followed by gateway glimpses of the river at its broadest and most majestic. Then a gap by the village school offered a glimpse of Exmouth across the water before I took the corner at School Hill junction and marched on to the thatched cottage and the leafy gardens and high hedges of up-market properties.

It was good to swing along through a fine morning for a change after so many wet winter days. I was in sweater, tracksuit trousers and climbing boots, and had the energy of a five-year-old – well, a forty-five year old.

A trio of shaggy ponies wearing long, Clint Eastwood raincoats, nodded silent greetings as I went by. Beyond them was a terrific view of Lyme Bay, the bottom of the sky alive with flocking birds and a raven laying its cry on the hush.

Des. res. succeeded des. res. and tall, wild hedges stood above dense verges. Then, at the bend, I could look down the long coombe to Dawlish Warren where houses and caravans sort of faded away to dunes, marram grass sand spits, river and sea.

Well, Nature takes a lot of kicks in the teeth from our species and it lifts me whenever I see it given the chance to do its own thing. On the other hand, if you want to rediscover the miraculous in the commonplace all you have to do is get out of the rut, get out of town and open your heart and eyes. Then, in a Devon lane, you may find the sun reduced to a twinkle on a thrush's beak and the magic of a primary school hymn in the skylark's song.

The lane climbed on between tall hedges, past Eastdon plantation. The way was sun dappled and I was squelching through leaf mulch and skirting big puddles before the route dropped towards a fabulous view. Ahead to the right, swept by cloud shadows, was the Vale of Dawlish and the tree-clad Haldon Hills. Standing at a gate I enjoyed the patchwork of small fields before walking on to the fork where I took the sharp left-hand turn into Orchard Lane, with Eastdon Plantation to the left and Eastdon Wood briefly on the right.

The descent brought me into another of those glorious visions of Dawlish Warren.

Presently, Eastdon Wood was replaced by open farmland. A shower fell and rain water streamed off the surface of the lane. Then the sun came out and I could look across the estuary to the coast. The houses on Exmouth's sea front were sunlit and the Warren lay low in the dark meeting of river and sea.

Walking down past thatch and old houses I came to the Dawlish Warren Road for an abrupt left turn. The railway embankment on the right hid the river but I don't suppose the occupants of Eastdon Farm Cottage, who had front row close-ups of BR's Intercity and Sprinter cabaret, minded. Morning and evening flights of wild geese and the piping of waders were also part of the show.

It was a busy road. Traffic moved at speed despite the floods at the bend, but the marvellous inertia of the scarecrows in the wayside fields kept my mind off the antics of some of the motorists who were probably off-duty Kamikaze pilots.

There were more scarecrows in the next field and a little later near Kenbury Crescent on the outskirts of Cockwood I could relax on the pavement and arrived safely back in the village.

The lovely little harbour was waiting at the bend with a few oystercatchers wading about in the low water slop. Of course I had to loiter with content before pushing on past the small houses, the Church Hall and The Anchor Inn, and swinging left into Church Road where the signpost read: Cofton.

Leaving the village stores behind me I opened the door of The Ship and went in. As far as cosy interiors go this one was five star. Regulars were resting their butts on stools at the bar and the lighting was soft enough for a Valentine's Day rendezvous.

John Crompton and Julie Culver run a friendly pub. The summer beer garden offers estuary views and the huge fireplace was one of those inn features that never fail to attract me whenever I enter a bar.

The Ship at Cockwood is an authentic victuallers' house dating from the 17th century, and tucked away in the south west corner are the original baker's ovens. The coombe in front of the pub was once a mile long creek that ceased to flood when the railway closed the entrance and Cockwood Harbour was built.

Cockwood marsh still floods but not high enough to stop locals dropping in for a chat, a pint and a game of darts. The dining area is a popular family haunt and it is Egon Ronay recommended.

For me pubs are still places where you can sit, drink and relax and enjoy a bit of company. A real Inn is much more than a glorified restaurant with booze licence. It's a combination of history and atmosphere, a touch of make-believe and warmth – human and otherwise.

— 3 —
The Day that the Rains Didn't Come Down
From the Old Coaching House, Chudleigh

(Through the lanes over the Kate Brook to Biddlecombe Cross, Waddon Barton, Brimley Corner and back across the Kate Brook to Chudleigh again – three miles)

Chudleigh lies just off the A38 Exeter–Plymouth road. If you do not intend to visit the pub at the end or beginning of the walk it would be sensible to park in the large free car park in the centre of the village.

UNBELIEVABLY the rain stopped before I left the car park at the Old Coaching House, the sun shone and I turned right to walk past Chudleigh's shops and pubs to Clifford Street.

The quiet little town had lost none of its appeal since I first came here in the 1950s to play soccer on the South Devon League circuit. In fact, in those days when hardly anybody I knew owned a car, the football coach trips introduced me to remote corners of coast, country and moors.

The Wheel, Chudleigh

Looking down on Chudleigh, a village set in glorious countryside

Not that soccer was on my mind as I swung right to stroll down the delightful narrows of Clifford Street where rows of little houses faced each other and the tiny Gospel Hall was closed. Ahead was a glimpse of the countryside to come,

Thatched cottages at Waddon

but I passed more small town cottages, some leafy properties and the Wheel Craft Workshop and restaurant before I crossed the bridge over the Kate Brook.

There was a bit of new housing development on the left, a row of houses, the cemetery, flail-mowed hedges and gateway views of hundreds of wet acres of farmland. I needed no reminder of the monsoon start to the year. Puddles, mud, flooded field corners, swollen streams and rivers, dripping trees – yes, it had been a wet old winter.

Bearing left beyond the barn conversions I came up the hill between tall hedges to Biddlecombe Cross. The drive leading to Lower Dunscombe Farm was on the right and I walked to a left hand turning signposted Exeter for the ridge view of fields, woodland, hills and coombes with the busy A38 down below to the right. Winter wheat gleamed, sparrows sniffled and sneezed, and a rabbit with a runny nose peered glumly up at the sky from the hedge top, wondering why raindrops weren't falling on its head like they had been since early December.

Then it was left once more down a narrow lane. Hazel catkins shook gently above ferny banks and sheep dotted the little fields as I passed Waddon Barton's collection of outbuildings and cottages. The roof on Waddon Thatch was old, the walls were white, the paintwork light blue, and the garden pond dreamed of the dragonflies summer would bring in.

A blackbird flapped through the frail February sunlight, dropped into a tree, flirted its tail and delivered a low key winter version of its spring aria. The timing couldn't have been better for I had arrived at another gate for one of those red soil panoramas no native Devonian could contemplate without a swelling of the heart.

The farmland rolled to the higher hills of the in-country and the dark sweep of moors with Hay Tor, Saddle Tor and Rippon Tor on the horizon. Huge clouds rolled across the landscape and I walked on to the bungalow and a gentle left hand turn at Brimley Corner.

It was comforting to look up every so often and see the tors in the bottom of the sky. It's no accident that Devon rhymes with heaven. A mole with bronchitis coughed and nodded his agreement.

The lane was narrow and wet, and it ran past a barn and the muddy corner of a field where two amiable pigs with glossy brown legs glanced up at me from

their trough. They had the nice open faces of retired primary school teachers or saints that had just discovered the world's best cider.

Chudleigh FC's pitch was on the right where the lane was returning me to the outskirts of the town by way of another little bridge spanning the Kate Brook.

Stone wall on one side, and hedge on the other saw me to the left turn into New Exeter Street. Here the pavement walking brought me by tiny cottages and town houses to the cenotaph and the last leg of the return to The Old Coaching House.

It was a weekday lunchtime and there was plenty of room in the spacious Long Bar. The atmosphere was friendly but not pushy, something reminiscent of certain hotels in the heart of London or the edge of mountain country. In practically every other sense the inn is huge with a dining area and facilities for Steak and Skittle parties.

There are low ceilings, oak beams, beer barrel tables, wooden settles and soft lighting from plenty of lamps. The fire was one of those big artificial jobs.

"It wouldn't pay to light the open fire throughout the winter," innkeeper Kath Staniforth told me. "We save them for Christmas and special occasions "

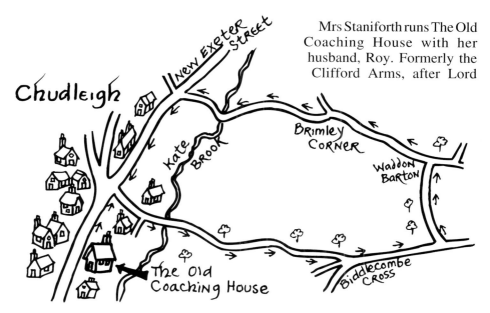

Mrs Staniforth runs The Old Coaching House with her husband, Roy. Formerly the Clifford Arms, after Lord Clifford the Chudleigh aristocrat who lived at Ugbrooke Park, The Old Coaching House is the sort of place to visit with a large group of friends. But I felt at home in a corner of the bar watching the waitresses come and go while I listened to the laughter of the people taking lunch.

— 4 —
A Stroll with Everything ... Except Tess!
From the Nobody Inn, Doddiscombsleigh

(Doddiscombsleigh, Tick Lane, Lakeham Farm, Willhayes Cross, Windy Cross, Lowley, Spanishlake Cross and Doddiscombsleigh again – seven miles)
Doddiscombsleigh is most easily reached from the top of Haldon Hill. Follow the ridge route past the Forestry Commission HQ at Bullers Hill. At Lawrence Castle (Belvedere) turn left and take next right after ⅓ mile.

I CAN hear the ghost of my old dad breathing his incredulity through the strings of his second-hand harp. But a walk from a pub and back to a pub isn't a pub crawl and a bar-fuelled hike certainly wasn't on my mind as I left the car park of the Nobody Inn and turned right to come through the spring sun haze.

Finches skipped along in the air before me, other birds sang and it only needed Tess of the Durbervilles to waltz round the corner to complete the Doddiscombsleigh rural idyll.

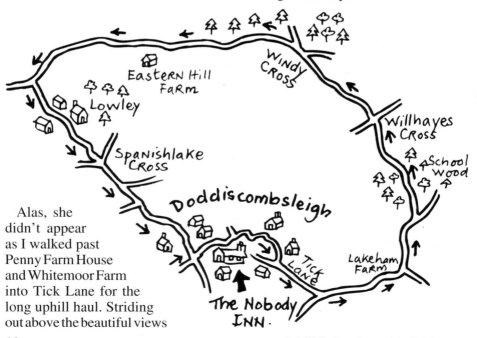

Alas, she didn't appear as I walked past Penny Farm House and Whitemoor Farm into Tick Lane for the long uphill haul. Striding out above the beautiful views

I couldn't understand why more people didn't go in for lane walks.

Cowley Brake's mature deciduous trees were a conservationist's bonus gratefully perceived as I swung left at the junction, signposted Chudleigh. A songthrush sang and the horses in the field nodded their approval while I marched on to Lakeham Farm.

The road looped up the hillside towards the vision of Lawrence Castle (Haldon Belvedere) which was wrapped in polythene and scaffolding, to the crossroads where my route left was signposted Exeter. Tower Wood was on the right and the views

Windy Cross

were hazy tree-shadowed, hills and fields. Cars swished by and I was walking between Webberton Wood and School Wood.

But it wasn't long before the great slopes of gorse and primrose banks were falling on the left into a vision of countryside lost in the blur of good weather.

Horseboxes stood in a field corner and the road wound up and down to Willhayes Cross where it was straight on, signed Longdown.

Looking towards Lowley

Everything combined to create a blend of past and present – spring sunshine, birdsong, tall wild hedges on the left; flail-mowed on the right. And maybe the village in the valley was Doddiscombsleigh. I didn't care. It was all very Hilaire Belloc with a touch of Edward Thomas and Yeats thrown in. The woodland was lovely, the gorse was gold and catkins danced above the view of the Teign Valley.

At Windy Cross I bore left for Christow although that village was far beyond my destination. To be honest I don't like this sort of discrepancy. Places should be signposted in sequence, so take note chaps and sharpen up your act.

Anyway, I was swinging along below Halsbeer Plantation. A robin sang as melodiously as ever and the low, lumpy hills were holding the sunlight on their curves. It was the sort of scene Hazlitt would have appreciated and maybe the downhill stretch past Easternhill Farm was classical west country. Great dollops of mud cobbled the lane and I was weaving along between mossy banks, primroses and bird cries.

At the crossroads it was left for Lowley which was all sorts of things – a wood and farmsteads, upper and lower. Piles of building bricks, old barns and byres brought me to the shocking pink building of Lower Lowley.

The way was narrow now, with grass in the middle. Crows rattled off at each other, larks sang and Lower Lowley stood out, literally, like a sore thumb.

Beyond Spanishlake Cross two turkeys strolled around a field near Lake Farm and a marvellous calm prevailed. Then there was a bungalow with horses looking over the half doors of stables and a couple of blackbirds quarrelling as I came past a wonderful old byre and Lower Greystone.

The way left was signposted Doddiscombsleigh, a cock crowed, hens banjoed

and more horses peered at me over stable doors. After Lake House it was all uphill in the sun towards the thatch, the church tower and the pub.

By any standards the Nobody Inn is special. Landlord Nick Borst-Smith was away on holiday but I was shown around by Dorothy, a member of his staff, who described herself cheerfully as the Nobody's dogsbody.

For nearly 25 years Mr Borst-Smith has built up the reputation of his 16th century inn and his cellar with its choice of 700 bottled wines is probably the best in the UK. And when you go in the lounge bar with its low ceiling and carved antique settles, chairs and benches, plus the carriage lamps, you'll be thinking about the 200 whiskies (mostly malts), and real ales and farm ciders.

The ales were Old Stoker, Nobody's and Bass, and the ciders were a real Devon celebration with Gray's farmhouse and Inch's Stonehouse which I sampled in the sort of relaxed atmosphere that would have tempted a teetotaller.

The Ringsdon Triangle
From the Dolphin Inn, Kenton

(Kenton, Clumpit Lane, Chiverstone Farm and Kenton again – three miles)
The best way to Kenton is along the A379, although you could negotiate the network of lanes above the village and come in the back way.

THE Dolphin Inn stands on the corner of the A379, Exeter Road, and Fore Street, in the little village of Kenton. That bright, windswept, sunny March afternoon it was laying its woodsmoke on the air as I set off from the car park next door and came up Fore Street past the War Memorial and All Saints Church which is a really impressive building.

Beyond Mamhead Road an eiderdown was hanging out to air from the bedroom window of an old house. In High Street the parade of red brick houses and low cottages with roofed doors brought me to the crossroads where my left turn was signposted Lyson, Oxton.

Soon I discovered that, as lane walks go this one was special. To start with, the hedge on the left had been carefully laid and the high bank facing it was etched with badger paths. The wind had nearly all the undergrowth in disarray and it was great to find stitchwort in flower and goose grass a lovely fresh shade of green as I pushed on into a countryside of small fields and copses. Haldon's woodland was high on the horizon ahead, the Obelisk prominent, and a brook ran through the coombe on the left below

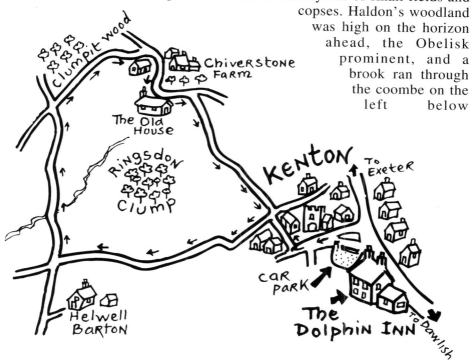

Helwell Barton. Small birds sang and wispy clouds drifted close to the sun whose pale gold was there, rain or shine, in the petals of the celandines.

Climbing the hill I paused to look back at Kenton church tower before the wild flowers on the bank and the fox and badger runs prompted a bit of Nature detective work.

I found red dead-nettle and the tiny white flowers of barren strawberry, with the odd oak towering over everything. The heavy rains had deposited drifts of silt and sand on the lane but a skylark was singing above the wayside field and spring was a definite presence.

The going was level now and at the crossroads my route to the right was signed Kenn and Exeter. It was a really gentle descent, the wind rushing through the tree tops and more badger runs and diggings in the hedgebank. Alas, the flail mower had got there ahead of me and maybe the old dead tree looking down on the mess was a kind of memorial to what might have been.

Apart from the rain-deposit sand in the lane there were little "beaches" of

The Triangle at Kenton

it in the field corners and a stream and a weir in the pasture at the bend. Sheep and lambs looked contented, a blackbird's nest was up in the hedgerow ivy, oak buds were out and I had reached the bridleway called Clumpit Lane where I met a nice old couple, Mr and Mrs Baker.

"This used to be Sandy Lane," Mrs Baker smiled as we were passed by a woman on a horse.

To the left stood the oaks of Clumpit Wood, with Ringsdon Clump on the right. Although

Pub Walks in and around the Haldon Hills

the hill is at the heart of the walk the copse at the top is sometimes out of sight.

A green woodpecker's cry followed me as I swung right at the junction and came along the narrow road between high banks into Chiverstone Farm. A dog was barking, outbuildings were catching the sun and daffodils were rocking in the cider apple orchard. The Old House standing under its thatch on the bend completed the rural idyll.

Kenton as seen from the side of Warboro Hill

Then it was good to walk up the winding lane with larks singing as Kenton Church tower came into view. A honey bee explored the daffodils on top of the bank and I was suddenly back at the crossroads on the edge of the village on my way through the narrows to the Dolphin.

Innkeeper, David Hatcher, had stocked up the wood burning stoves and I sat over a Guinness in the Nook bar. The pub is a real warren of alcoves and intimate little corners where families can hole up and enjoy the pleasant, Dickensian gloom.

There are also Nook Dining Rooms, lots of wooden settles and the main bar with its huge range and wood burning stove, dart boards and pool tables. Here the atmosphere was that blend of past and present typical of the best village pubs.

The nook stoves are central to the old pub's appeal. When I began the walk their smoke was on the breeze and it was great to end the hike sitting on a stool before the glow of the logs that were creating that rural smell.

— 6 —
The Beauty of Nature in the Brewing
From the Swan Inn, Dawlish

(Dawlish, Ashcombe Road, Lower Rixdale, Radfords, Luscombe and Dawlish again – three miles)
When you get to Dawlish ask for Old Town Street and the Swan Inn.

THE daffodils brightened a dull morning as I left the car park of The Swan in Old Town Street and came up Weech Road past Old Badlake House and its thatched roof. Then it was the kind of edge of town walking I enjoy with yesteryear's forge among other architecture on a human scale.

At Aller Hill I swung right, signposted Ashcombe, and took the bend left into Ashcombe Road which is really a glorified lane. Not that I'm complaining. The countryside above The Brook – sorry, Dawlish Water – had begun immediately and was South Devon at its most intimate.

The lane was wet. It ran between tall hedgebanks until it was suddenly dry and I could stop body swerving around puddles and enjoy the gateway "windows" on a farmland of small woods and fields. Properties were partially hidden by hedges, cattle chomped away in a pasture and I was walking up a gentle hill with a blackbird flying ahead of me. Celandine gold gleamed from the hedge bottoms and daffodils stood to attention on top of the wall outside the house called Littlestone.

Looking down the valley towards Dawlish

Nearby a couple of lambs were cuddled together on some hay in the corner of a wet field. It was the last day of February, the tiny white flowers of stitchwort were out and a lark was singing over winter wheat.

A bit further on I swung sharp left and came down to Dawlish Water. The stream was swollen but even if the footbridge hadn't been there the water was only ankle deep at the ford.

Then the lane laid on snowdrops, bracket fungi at the base of trees, and gaunt farm machinery in a field above the hedge. Mud and water gleamed but despite the greyness there was the feel of impending spring in the air. Countryside brewing its own quiet beauty, with winter coming to an end, usually manages to make me optimistic. All the life to come in birth, bud, blossom and birdsong can't be denied. The celandines in the hedges echoed this.

At the next bend stood the huge granite gateposts of Lower Rixdale, a lovely old red-walled farm. A dog barked and sheep and their lambs were motionless in the pasture beside Dawlish Water.

Lower Dawlish Water Lane wound on, gently upwards, and small birds continued to throw snatches of song at me. And as I walked I knew that soon all those bits and pieces of hedgerow music would blur to the magic of the dawn chorus.

The rural complex further on was called Radfords. Old farm buildings and big Pitt House registered like monuments to yesterday's agricultural scene. Woodsmoke rose from the chimney of one of the red brick cottages opposite Combe Brook, a large cream house. Peering over the well on the left I saw tiny Christmas trees in pots or beds, and beyond the conifer garden free range chickens free ranged.

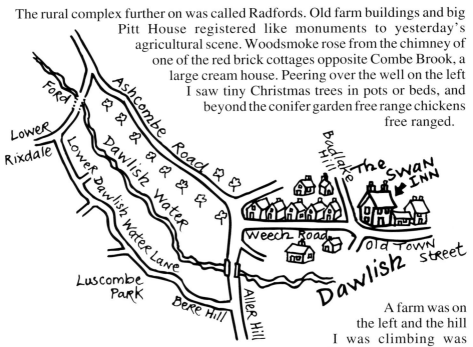

A farm was on the left and the hill I was climbing was littered with straw. Over the low hedge I could look into the coombe where Dawlish Water flowed. I must say, though, that I prefer the local name for the stream – The Brook.

The big house on the right was probably the old convent, and these references to the past were a bit sad if you've lived in South Devon all your life, with a wartime childhood thrown in. Then I was loping past old stone walls, moss and ferns, and some lovely deep pink thatched cottages with roofed doors, just down from the crossroads where I had swung left, signposted Dawlish.

A blackbird on a branch saluted me as I walked on down Bere Hill below Luscombe Park to Aller Hill, the next crossroads and another left turn, ignoring the Smallacombe Farm sign. Presently I was crossing the bridge over the Brook to retrace my steps along Weech Road back to the Swan Inn.

Coming in the back way I saw the beer garden and a grassy patch, planted with fruit trees, sloping above it. Ed and Liz McLaughlin are justly proud of that small green corner.

I sampled a half of Guinness in the small public bar which has an open fire, dart board, homely tables and chairs, and limited-edition rugby prints on the walls. The lounge was just as attractive with its wood burning stove.

The Swan is a real pub, a place which would have got the nod of approval from my dad.

Its charm owes much to the marriage of past and present and the vision of the McLaughlins. It really is the village pub on the edge of town.

— 7 —
Morning of the Marram
From The Mount Pleasant Inn, Dawlish Warren

(Mount Pleasant Road, Beach Way, Greenland Lake, Outer Warren, The Bight, Warren Point and the Shore back – three miles)
Take the A379 road and either turn off at Cockwood or at Dawlish into the road that leads to the Warren. The Mount Pleasant is sited at the top of the steep slope that runs from the entrances to the main car parks.

THE Mount Pleasant is a big pub in Dawlish's holidayland where both tourism and wildlife enjoy the benefits of the Gulf Stream. Well, I couldn't have chosen a finer Sunday morning but instead of asking the innkeeper if I could use his car park I was chauffeur-driven down Mount Pleasant Road past Dron Lodge and along Beach Road which is the direct route to Dawlish Warren.

My friends parked in the main car park on the far side of the railway bridge, and I was ejected to do my own thing. The sky was brilliant blue and the sun was as bright as the gleam in Romeo's eye. No wonder the car park was half full even though spring was more than a week away.

Wordsworth said: 'All things that love the sun are out of doors' and he was right. Parents, kids, young couples and lifelong mates were getting ready for a dose of the dunes.

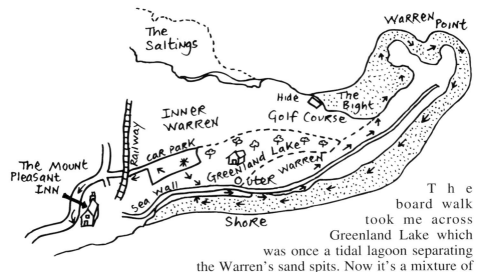

The board walk took me across Greenland Lake which was once a tidal lagoon separating the Warren's sand spits. Now it's a mixture of scrub, brambles and reeds, a place where you can see the celebrated Warren Crocus, a tiny lilac-blue flower that comes out in April and grows nowhere else on the UK mainland.

Among the other Greenland plants are the wild orchids and evening primroses, but the only things out when I came up onto the dunes of the Outer Warren were people – and birds.

The 505 acres of the reserve area of international importance and over the last 7,000 years various parts of it have been adopted by thousands of plants and 180 species of birds, from waders, ducks and geese to chiff chaffs and peregrines.

The double sandpit reaches out from the western side of the Exe into the

Estuary opposite the seaside town of Exmouth. The Nature Reserve incorporates The Saltings, the Inner Warren, Greenland Lake, Outer Warren, Pole Sands, Orcombe Point, bits of the golf course, and the shore.

There are Mobile Dunes where the sand will continue to shift until the marram grass turns them into Fixed Dunes.

The marram's leaves catch the sand and its intricate and expansive root system holds it. But this is a walk not a conservation lecture, and there are plenty of well written scientific books dealing with most aspects of the Warren.

Walkers and anglers shared the shore but I was content to stroll along the prom to the dunes and on towards that lovely low lying view of Exmouth. The waters of Lyme Bay were to the right, with Greenland Lake's turk, freshwater ponds, scrub willow and reeds to the left. Here and there the golf course intruded.

One of the most moving aspects of the route I had chosen were the sky larks

rising on their songs. There were dozens of them. Ducks lisped and a cold wind made the marram hiss; but the larks sang on ... and on and on, like angels.

Leaving the dunes I dropped down to the left at the bay called The Bight where lots of Brent Geese, ducks and waders feed. But the tide was out and small numbers of geese were barely visible on the water's edge and the distant sand bars of the estuary.

Larksong saw me across the bare mud to the sandy stretch which took me to the northern arm of Warren point for a beautiful view up river and Exmouth across the tidal surge. All the seafront villas stood out in hologram 3D.

I came right, round the point, to walk the soft sand towards Dawlish. Small flocks of Brent Geese flighted in, oystercatchers piped and dunlin were also on the move against the sun dazzle on the sea. Larksong and gull cries mingled, waves broke and people's dogs danced away from the aprons of foam.

Ahead red sandstone beckoned from Langstone to the cliffs beyond Dawlish. But I could see as far as Berry Head and the sky was misty blue now, with more than a hint of spring in it. If this was one of the scrumpy-puggled myths my Dad used to peddle in the public bar of his local, I would have been hurdling the wooden barriers called groynes which were built at right angles on the beach to prevent the sand being washed away. But I wasn't an Olympic star.

I climbed one here, ducked under one there or dodged around the end between waves. Then I nipped up onto the prom to watch the kite flyers and the marvellous inertia of the anglers before returning to the car park and the last leg to The Mount Pleasant Inn.

The pub was filling rapidly when I stood at the bar and waited for the Liffey Water to be poured. The tables in the Warren Bar window were all reserved, and understandably so. The view of the Warren, the Estuary and the sea must rank among the best in the South West.

While folk ate and drank, pool was being played in the pool room and an Intercity cut across the vision of dunes, river and Lyme Bay. It was the sort of cabaret a lot of pubs would envy. But it wasn't new to innkeeper Wally Protheroe who runs the Mount Pleasant with his wife June and son Malcolm.

Wally has been at the pub's helm for ten years and the crowded bars were a testament to his success and the place's popularity. Even the lounge bar upstairs was busy and you don't have to be Sherlock Holmes to put this down to the View-with-the-Brew magic.

Scenery apart, though, at the Mount Pleasant you have a choice of three or four ales and a couple of ciders plus everything else from kegs, bottles and optics.

But the Guinness was enough for me and I brought it to the terrace beer garden above that marvellous view. The sun took the sting out of the wind and the terror tot sitting with his mum and dad at the next table was trying to gouge the eyes out of an expressionless teddy bear. Yep, the Mount Pleasant cabaret has many acts.

WALKS IN THE SOUTH HAMS
Brian Carter

Brian encounters a kingdom of cider, brooks of bubbling barley wine, hidden hamlets, a wealth of wildlife, a festival of flora, colourful country characters and hospitable hostelries. Described in his own poetic style, here are a number of walks ranging in length from one mile up to a full day excursion of about eleven miles. Why not get your boots on and follow in Brian's footsteps to discover, for yourself, the quiet delights of the South Hams.

PUB WALKS IN THE SOUTH HAMS
Brian Carter

The South Hams is a magic corner of Britain where the towns are small and the countryside is big. The pubs match up to the scenery, from the red soil locals on the shores of Start Bay to the tucked-away inns pickled in history. Brian Carter is a novelist and artist whose love affair with the South Hams has lasted a lifetime. Follow in his footsteps or simply sit back and enjoy the colourful descriptions which will bring the splendour of the South Hams countryside to the comfort of your own home.

AROUND & ABOUT THE HALDON HILLS – REVISITED
Chips Barber

This book was the first ever written by Chips and was published in 1982. Since then there have been many changes, some for the better, some not. In this new up-dated edition the book follows the original format but also features new or amended material. The Haldon Hills remain a magical place so if you want to learn about the treacle mines, flying trains, a sylvan Francis Drake, sweet epitaphs, duelling doctors, murderous monks and beautiful bigamists, then this is the book to reveal all!

**For further details of these or any of our Devon titles, please contact
Obelisk Publications, 2 Church Hill, Pinhoe, Exeter EX4 9ER, tel: 01392 468556**